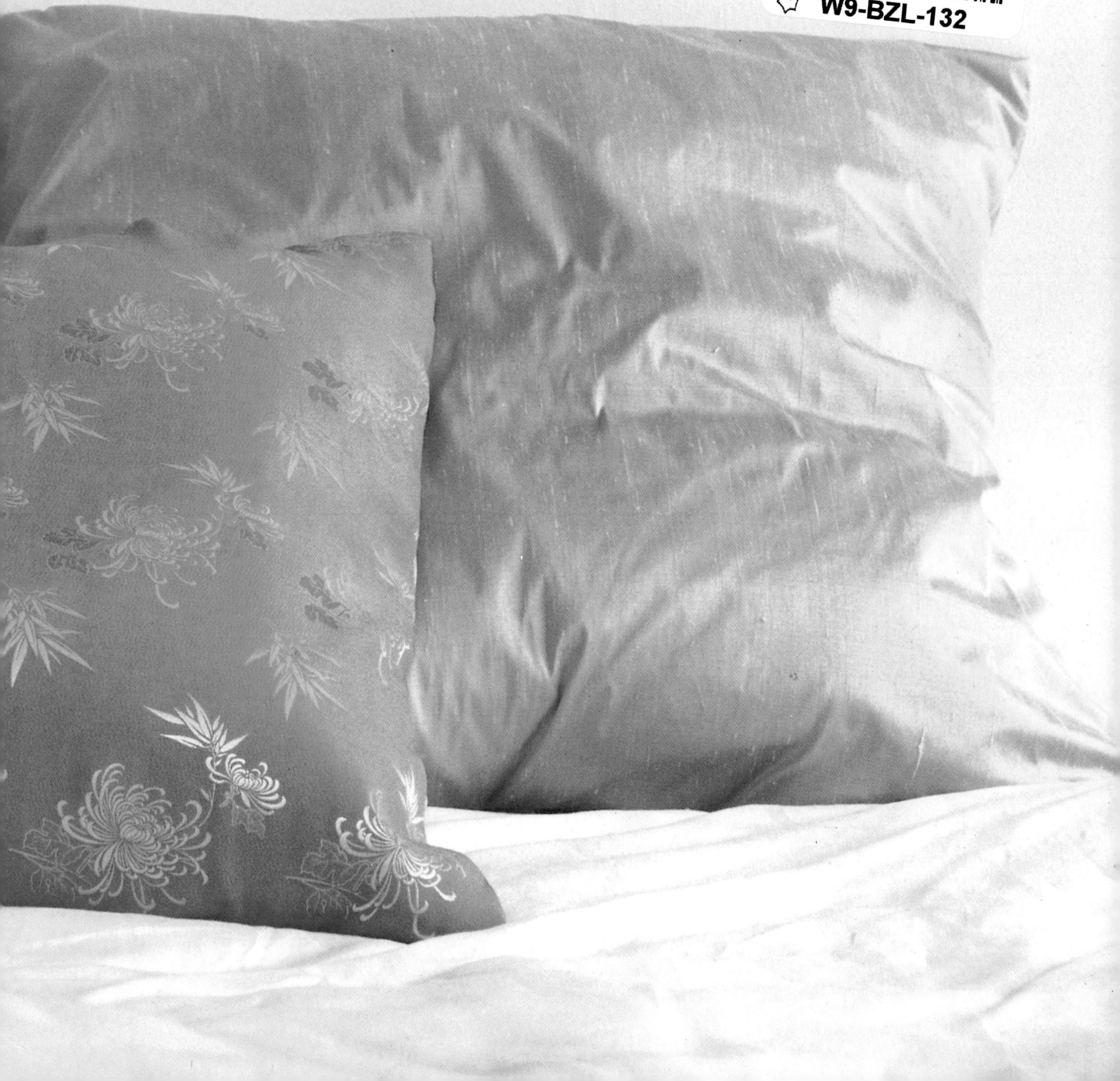

the relaxed home

the relaxed home

Atlanta Bartlett

photography by Polly Wreford

RYLAND
PETERS
& SMALL
LONDON NEW YORK

To David

Designer   Vicky Holmes
Senior editor   Hilary Mandleberg
Location research   Kate Brunt, Sarah Hepworth
Production   David Meads
Art director   Gabriella Le Grazie
Publishing director   Anne Ryland

Text contributor   Alice Westgate

First published in the U. S. in 2000 as *The Comforts of Home*
This new edition published in 2002 by Ryland Peters & Small
519 Broadway
5th Floor
New York, NY 10012
www.rylandpeters.com

Text © Atlanta Bartlett 2000
Design and photographs
© Ryland Peters & Small 2000

10 9 8 7 6 5 4 3 2 1

ISBN 1 84172 310 X

Printed and bound in China

contents

Light, fresh, and airy rooms, stamped with your own unique personality and untrammeled by conventional decorating styles such as minimalism or the ethnic look, are what relaxed living is all about. It is an approach that allows you to prop a huge carved and gilded period mirror against the wall of a room that also contains a classic fifties chair and chrome-legged coffee table. It even gives you the freedom to choose between paring down the decoration of a room to nothing and introducing just a bright floral dress or cardigan to make a uniquely personal, if temporary, focal point, or luxuriating in layers of throws and cushions piled high on a welcoming sofa.

introduction

If you are the sort of person who adores comfort and revels in the freedom to do your own thing, then you will love *The Comforts of Home*. Its warm, easygoing looks offer a more livable alternative to the stark, minimalist interiors popular in recent years. But "livable" does not mean lacking in style. In fact, many of the trends seen in *The Comforts of Home*—feminine florals and floaty fabrics decorated with sequins and beads, for instance—have come straight off the fashion runway. *The Comforts of Home* brings these trends into your house, making them up-to-the-minute without being shallow, pretty without being cloying, glamorous without being intimidating, stylish without being impractical.

The relaxed approach to decorating allows your home to reflect your passions and interests. It encompasses everything from family photos, holiday memorabilia, and eccentric ornaments to vintage clothing, flowery china, and piles of books. There is scope, too, for splashes of glorious color and heartwarming texture— mohair, silk, velvet, and linen; wood, rattan, and leather.

And because *The Comforts of Home* offers an unstructured, carefree look, you can alter the decoration of your rooms as you please to reflect your changing tastes and needs. It is so easy to move furniture that is on casters, to replace a curtain that is no more than a fabric panel, to reposition a picture that simply leans

against a wall, to add new elements to a kitchen that is unfitted, to give a fresh new look to a sofa that is covered with a throw.

You can achieve a relaxed home through five different yet related approaches. Relaxed Simplicity is the pure, distilled face of relaxed living, while Relaxed Romantic shows you its floral, feminine side. Relaxed Sensuality gives you the excuse to indulge in an array of different textures, colors, scents, and shapes; but if you want a more sophisticated look and a touch of class, choose Relaxed Elegance. Finally there is Relaxed Eclectic—idiosyncratic and humorous, it is the look to opt for if you love many different things and your cabinets are full of impulse buys.

Think relaxed whenever you are decorating, and you will quickly see how the tired old clichés that may have constrained you previously become a thing of the past, and how spontaneity and individuality take their place. This is true in any room, from welcoming, comfortable living rooms, dining rooms, and kitchens to the intimate indulgences of bedrooms and bathrooms, and from creative but fun workspaces to stress-beating outdoor rooms.

And then it is up to you—now is your chance to interpret the relaxed look in your own way and bring to it your own inimitable style. For unless your home has your unique personality at its heart, it cannot ever be said to be truly and utterly comfortable.

left Whatever your passion—reading, hoarding beautiful stationery, collecting clothing made from sumptuous fabrics—relaxed living offers you an approach to decorating your home that allows you to put your favorite things center stage.

right In the relaxed home, rooms always have a welcoming feel, no matter how pared-down they are. A single flower in a glass and a brightly colored throw over the back of a chair bring a touch of warmth to starkly functional fifties furniture in a cool, minimalist room.

the relaxed look

relaxed
simplicity

All it takes to give a coolly pared-down room a sense of softness, warmth, and livability is an injection of heart-gladdening color and one or two sublimely lovely objects. This is simplicity at its most relaxed.

Simple interiors are often thought of as minimalist. But while minimalism might make you think of sparsely furnished, lofty rooms with severe, monochromatic color schemes—the kind of spaces that have now become something of a decorating cliché—the simply decorated rooms of the relaxed home have a far warmer and more livable character. They may have their roots in minimalism insofar as they are free of clutter and their decorative elements are usually of the pared-down variety, but

add shocking pink for bold contrast

they are nevertheless gently mellow places where softness and comfort are key, places where people feel a sense of welcome.

But there is more to this look than merely a late-nineties reaction to minimalism. The beauty of relaxed simplicity lies in the fact that you have the opportunity to soften the minimalism and inject your own sense of individuality into a room by introducing one or two things you are passionate about—maybe an exotically colored fabric or a richly textured throw—without spoiling the look's characteristic unfussiness. So when you fall in love with that piece of shocking pink Chinese silk, you can feel free to make it into a cushion cover and display it as a splash of color against a plain, white-upholstered daybed. You can soften the lines of an unpainted wooden chair by draping it with a length of beautifully muted vintage floral fabric. Or you can throw a nubbly woolen blanket over a low Japanese-style bed to introduce a little luxury.

cool, light, simple blues

Relaxed simplicity relies on having something in every room that is personal and well loved, something that makes a statement and gives the room impact. What are the objects that bring you happiness? Which are the colors that make your heart sing? What makes you feel at ease? You may choose something with an appealing texture, something strikingly colored or attractively patterned. But the crucial thing to remember is that, to keep the look simple, you need only one, or two at the most, of these decorative items. Use more and the effect will be diminished.

far left In a simple bedroom where pillows take the place of a headboard, color is the focal point. One shocking pink Chinese silk pillow adds sparkling contrast to an otherwise cool blue and white scheme.

right and below Magenta orchids are the only adornment on an uncluttered dressing table.

above left Touches of pink and lilac warm up a simple—verging on stark—living room. The fifties armchair and surfboard-design coffee table give the space a wonderfully retro feel.

above right Tall floor-to-ceiling windows allow daylight to flood into the room. The airy look is enhanced by pale wood floorboards and tiles. Although the furnishings are the embodiment of simplicity, the room still feels welcoming.

As for the other elements you introduce into the room, bear in mind the fact that the style of furniture you choose is hugely important to the look. The good news, though, is that relaxed rooms do not require expensive furniture. In fact, an old sofa, junk-shop table, or secondhand store fixtures will be more at home in this environment than a priceless antique crystal chandelier or a refined gilt and marble console table.

But whether you are starting completely from scratch or furnishing a room with items you already own, the secret of creating simple, relaxed rooms is to choose pieces with "good bones"—those that are characterized by slender, linear shapes and clean lines rather than bold, chunky styles. Think fifties tables on narrow tapering legs or graceful, slightly spare-looking armchairs with plain, unfussy wooden feet. These pieces not only look crisp and streamlined but also show the maximum amount of floor space beneath and surrounding—an important factor, given that a sense of spaciousness is another of the qualities to aim for.

As for color, it is a powerful decorating tool. It can bring a sense of unity to a busy room or can contribute an essential burst of vitality to a room that is lacking in interest. You also probably want to use a favorite color in your home, a color that evokes many memories and emotions. However, since the advent of minimalism, you might be tempted to imagine that simple rooms should be decorated only in pure white or neutral shades such as cream, stone, taupe, or parchment. But you will find that, with care, it is perfectly possible for you to use really bright colors in relaxed simple rooms without compromising the rooms' innate simplicity.

soften those classic fifties lines with flowers and fabric

Once you have decided on your favorite color, consider painting it on just one wall. Surround it with lots of white on the woodwork and even on the floors, then leave the wall free of pictures, so as not to detract from the color's decorative quality. In this way, the color itself will become your favorite thing, your focal point in the midst of otherwise pared-down, unadorned surroundings. And what could be simpler than that?

above For simplicity's sake, keep flower arrangements as uncluttered as possible. Choose a single flower head for dramatic impact and display it in a plain glass container. A guelder rose looks very effective on its own, as then its complex form can best be appreciated.

left What is more evocative than freshly gathered garden roses? Displayed in a glass tumbler, they add color to a white mantelshelf. Personalize the display by combining the roses with a selection of family photographs and a framed selection of pebbles brought back from a seashore vacation. Together they will bring back lovely memories of happy times.

above In a distinctly minimalist corner of a room, the fluid lines of a modern classic chair of molded plywood are decoration enough. To let the chair be appreciated fully, all the other decorative elements—the earthy tone of the walls and the wooden floorboards—are kept as low-key as possible.

right Contrast is the secret here, as the strong, dark lines of the hand-crafted wooden vase and bowls throw the pure-white-painted fireplace into relief. Such dramatic arrangements—based on just one or two of the owner's favorite things—are a quick and simple way to transform an unexciting room.

left, above Create a blisfully simple still life by displaying two old glass bottles alongside some scrap metal collected for its color and textural interest. Soften the scheme by adding a length of old white linen draped along the mantel.

left, below A worn old denim jacket and a fine pashmina shawl hanging against a plain white wall create a visual feast with a wonderfully relaxed pairing of opposites.

this picture The owner of this old Parisian apartment exposed the original beams to add textural and visual interest to the white walls of an otherwise simple bedroom.

relaxed
romantic

Paint a room in the coolest ice-cream colors, furnish it with the simplest beds and chairs, add a restrained helping of sun-faded floral fabrics, beads, and flowers, and you have the recipe for today's relaxed romantic look.

Twenty years ago, if you had asked a designer to create a romantic interior, the chances are you would have ended up with a mass of period frills, flounces, and flowers. These frothy, visually complex schemes are the antithesis of modern, pared-down interiors, so it might surprise you to find that romanticism plays a role in today's relaxed homes.

There is, of course, a crucial difference. Relaxed romanticism takes a conventionally romantic touch—a floral fabric, a beaded throw, or a soft pastel paint shade—and places it in a restrained, often minimalist setting. The result is a distillation of conventional romanticism, producing a thoroughly modern feel that is appropriate in any room in the house.

Femininity and theatricality are both part of the mood. Now is definitely the time to give free rein to all those impulsive

One of the most beautiful ways of adding a dash of romance and pattern to any pared-down room is to introduce some delicate floral material, preferably on a white or off-white background. You could try using a flowery throw over the arm of a simple chair or sofa, or one or two dainty floral-patterned cushions to soften the look of a modern steel bed. The bedroom is the ideal place to introduce a piece of vintage clothing. No matter that it is never worn, a floral fifties evening dress draped casually over a dressing-table stool readily becomes part of the room's decoration.

use **dreamy florals**
but in moderation

nothing could be more romantic
than floral fabrics in the bedroom

decorative touches you thought were well and truly out of bounds in the contemporary home. That thirties dress or drop-dead gorgeous kimono that caught your eye at a flea market can become part of your decorating scheme, rather than something you end up stowing away in a closet. It doesn't matter if you never wear them; owning them and showing them off is satisfying in itself. Display them on sturdy wooden hangers against a wall like works of art, and change them with the seasons or according to your mood.

Costume jewelry and theatrical-looking accessories can serve as decoration, too. Strands of glittery beads and pretty necklaces look fabulous draped over the corner of a picture frame; a pile of brooches in a glass dish might be the only adornment a plain white-painted mantelpiece needs; a collection of

Color is a major factor when it comes to creating a relaxed romantic decor, and sugared-almond pinks and mauves fill the bill perfectly. See how a beautifully tactile lilac beaded throw can soften the effect of a white-painted table and how a number of different fabrics—jacquards, floral prints, and quilted cottons—in closely related shades have more impact when used together than when scattered around a room. A simple bunch of flowers adds a touch of romance whatever the occasion.

glamorously sexy satin shoes can be turned into a focal point with a difference; a cane mannequin generously festooned with necklaces becomes an object of desire, especially when it is standing on a delicate gilded metal console table.

Flowery fabrics, once spurned for being overly sentimental, are again big news, and many textile manufacturers have reissued old designs to capture the new romantic mood. This time around, though, the look is altogether fresher and simpler. The trick is

shine on in gilt, glass, and satin

to use restraint. A flowery pillow cover or a single chair covered in informal, softly billowing chintz is all you need. Choose muted and simple colors, preferably with a white or neutral background, and make sure that the rest of the room is not fighting for attention. Walls should be painted in neutral colors or soft pastels; furniture should have simple, uncomplicated lines.

Nostalgia for the past immediately conjures up romance and so is another key influence in this relaxed look. Wherever you can, use sun-faded fabrics, old-fashioned alarm clocks, squishy sofas, roll-top bathtubs, and old cut-glass vases instead

of their modern equivalents. But whereas twenty years ago it would have been *de rigueur* to display these items in rooms decorated in a heavy pastiche of a past style, now they should be set alongside minimalist white walls and white-painted floors.

For in the relaxed romantic interior, freshness, lightness, wit, and irreverence have replaced slavish coordination and tired old historical clichés. Romance is there at every turn, but this newly minted version is sparkling, lively, and never cloyingly sentimental.

opposite An assortment of vintage beads and costume jewelry bought at fairs and flea markets introduces elements of theatricality and nostalgia as well as romance.

above Surround yourself with your favorite things. These drop-dead gorgeous shoes have an almost sculptural quality when arranged on an old gilded screen.

above right For a display that allows you to revel in the quintessential romance of florals, simply leave a flower-encrusted evening bag lying on a chintz-covered armchair.

right A wicker dressmaker's dummy draped with quirky costume jewelry prevents a gilded table and mirror from appearing overly formal.

relaxed
sensuality

When you long to indulge your senses of sight, smell, and touch, choose relaxed sensuality and surround yourself with a wealth of richly varied colors, fabrics, shapes, textures, and patterns.

far left Rumpled yet luxurious. Richly embroidered bed linen and satin pillowcases epitomize today's relaxed sensuality.

left In relaxed rooms, furniture and accessories do not always have to be used for the purpose for which they were intended. Here a sari hangs at the window to diffuse the light and cast a colored glow. The sensuous effect is heightened by the juxtaposition with the austere—white-painted floorboards, a retro-style chrome cart and lamp, and an old-fashioned radiator.

below A bed below a sunny window is perfect for an afternoon nap. Yet again, the sensuous element—a gold-embroidered cushion cover—contrasts sharply with simplicity—the crisp white bed linen beneath.

Relaxed simplicity and relaxed romantic are characterized by the beauty of their restraint. Their hallmark is their specially selected decorative touches here and there amid otherwise fairly low-key surroundings. There may be times, however, when you feel like being a little less self-disciplined, when you long to indulge yourself and create a more complex interior. Rather than limiting yourself to one or two tasteful objects in a room, you might yearn to include a profusion of your favorite things.

freshly fuchsia

Think relaxed sensuality and you immediately have a theme that, with the greatest subtlety, will provide the link you need to bring all the different elements together. With relaxed sensuality, you can appeal not only to the sense of sight but also to the senses of touch and smell. Relaxed sensuality gives you the excuse to introduce more than one color into a room, to put a rich array of patterns next to one another, to mix contrasting textures, even to capitalize on the scent of

far left The details are simple but the effect is sensuous. Create it yourself with layers of rich colors for bedding, wall hangings, and even book covers. Use shades of hot pink, red, and orange for a sense of enveloping warmth and comfort.

left Tactile embroidered and ruched fabrics look even more spectacular alongside dainty florals.

right An intricate earring artlessly laid on a mantel demonstrates how the unexpected can become part of your interior decoration.

seasonal flowers to add atmosphere. Decorate a whole house like this, and it will be overbearing, but make just one room really sensuous, the rest restrained, and the contrast will prove stunning.

Start by indulging the sense of sight—the most important of the five senses for interior decorating. Introduce a riot of deep colors—sexy pinks, burnt umbers, sultry purples,

left The simplest touches—sunshine and fresh air coming in at an open window and a jam jar of delicate bluebells on the table—are enough to boost your sense of well-being and make you feel your senses are being indulged.

above right For extra sensory richness, feast your eyes on small pleasures such as colored hand-painted glassware and vividly patterned ceramics.

below right Use sensuous details sparingly and they will have even more impact. Fresh flower heads heaped on a plate bring a splash of color to a room, as well as sweet fragrance. Choose beautiful orchids for out-and-out exoticism.

far right The elegant sweep of this curved staircase reveals how even your home's architectural elements can provide a sensuous dimension.

or exotic turquoises. Let saturated blues and greens transport you to the seashore.

Introduce these colors on walls, then enrich the visual feast with an assortment of throws, curtains, cushions, lamps, and flowers. Combine closely related tints—think ocher and brown with terra cotta or shocking pink, brick red with burnt orange—to give a feeling of intimacy. Or put together vividly contrasting shades—turquoise with lilac or cerise, lime green with orange—to surprise and revitalize.

But why leave your perfume in the bedroom? If you do not have honeysuckle growing outside your window or a tangy sea breeze wafting in through an open door, then improvise with a vase of perfumed fresh flowers, a bowl of rose petals, or a smoldering incense stick.

Once you start to nourish your senses you will quickly realize how they can add another dimension to your life. So harness their power and bring them into every room of the house to create relaxed sensuality.

note the details, nourish the senses

With relaxed sensuality you can happily put rich textures against a vibrant background; keep this in mind when selecting everything from fabrics and flooring to furniture and work surfaces. Introduce ceramic tiles, marble, wood, brick, or metal. Go to town with a range of fabrics that feel wonderfully sensuous—silks and satins, velvets, cashmere, suede, and tweed. And since textured materials have their own inherent patterns, by using them you will be appealing to the sense of sight as well as to the sense of touch.

As for the sense of smell, it is well known that scent and sensuality go hand in hand.

relaxed
elegance

Put a lavish, carved bed in an understated bedroom, a fifties glass vase in a grand hallway, and you have relaxed elegance—the sophisticated, glamorous face of today's relaxed living.

Relaxed elegance has an underlying glamour. It is the grown-up face of relaxed living—the style to adopt if you want just a hint of formality. Tailor-made for lofty rooms with high ceilings, molded cornices, and generous windows, relaxed elegance is opulent but modern and measured, so it can be surprisingly effective in contemporary settings, too.

The look begins with the main items of furniture, and for relaxed elegance you really do need one or two breathtaking pieces. This is where it will pay you to look around antique markets and secondhand furniture stores. If you are lucky enough to find an intricately carved turn-of-the century wooden bed, for example, you will transform an ordinary bedroom into a ravishing boudoir. In the same way, an original seventies sofa and matching

unique period pieces set the tone but are not overpowering

Relaxed elegance demands an injection of grandeur and glamour in otherwise simple, contemporary rooms. In this bedroom, highly polished floorboards speak of traditional country-house sophistication in a way that bleached or colorwashed boards would not. A classic carved French bed draped with luxury fabrics and a big vase of freshly gathered flowers continue the theme. Notice how the bed's carving is the room's only concession to ornament and how the plainness of its surroundings emphasize its intricacy.

chairs will bring a touch of class to a living area, while a single gilded chair will give even the most modest corner ideas above its station. And you can never go wrong with a daybed or chaise longue—both are the epitome of elegant self-indulgence. Splurge on one or two pieces like these, and they will do most of the hard work for you, creating a sense of glamour in one stroke. Meanwhile, keep the rest of the furniture simple to insure that understatement rules and the balance does not tip toward ostentation.

plain and simple backdrops offset by lavish accessories

To prevent relaxed elegance from becoming over-the-top opulence, the secret is to keep the background clean and simple. With off-white walls and woodwork and understated yet generously proportioned sofas, a room can easily handle a dramatic gilded mirror, an ornate period wall clock, and piles of cushions covered in velvets and sari silks.

right and above There is no need to feel that elegance can be found only in conventional "period" pieces. Items from the sixties are now enjoying a comeback and appear in the relaxed home in many different guises. Here a couple of pieces of vivid retro glassware make a surprisingly successful combination with a more traditionally elegant console table and mirror. The idea of juxtaposing the unusual continues with the addition of a simple modern, unframed black and white photograph.

opposite Mantelpiece arrangements do not have to follow a conventional formula, either. An elegant period teacup with a modern glass vase in clashing colors is a successful arrangement.

Decorate using colors associated with the elegance of past ages—a palette of delicate celadon green, olive, cream, and dreamy sky blue—then continue the elegant theme with sumptuous fabrics: ultra-soft velvets or chunky corduroys on everything from armchairs to cushion covers and generously draped window treatments. Alternatively, use lighter weight fabrics, but in abundance. Muslin curtains flowing onto the floor in generous folds or chairs swathed in yards of linen are less costly but still look lavish. And instead of gentle florals, choose plain, sophisticated fabrics in light shades.

Complement everything with polished parquet or wood floors and elegant lighting. Delicately shaded and gilded wall lights or secondhand crystal chandeliers, perhaps with painted rather than gilded brackets, make just the right statement.

Finally, underline the mood with your choice of accessories. A gently ticking antique clock on an otherwise empty mantelpiece, a fine glass vase filled with orchids on a decorative metal side table, a soft pashmina shawl used as a throw—all these small touches add understated opulence. Feel the glamour, but stay cool—and always utterly relaxed.

relaxed
eclectic

Flaunt your magpie instinct and make the most of the relaxed home's laid-back and wholly unassuming background by embellishing it with beautiful displays of all the things you love.

far left Old fabrics tend to have far more character than their modern mass-produced equivalents. Their faded colors and soft, worn texture mean that they are very much at home in a relaxed interior.

left and below Combine elements from around the world to create rooms that are truly eclectic. A decorative Japanese bottle or the simplest oriental dish and lacquered chopsticks broaden the horizons and add a touch of the exotic.

opposite The contents of your closet are bound to reflect your character and passions. With relaxed eclectic, you can put it all on show and make it part of your room's decor. It does not matter if you have a penchant for shoes, a craving for vintage clothing, or a thirst for ethnic pieces. They will all help project your individuality.

geisha girl and southern belle
make a heady mixture

In today's fast-moving world the media are constantly bombarding us with all the latest trends in fashion and interior decoration. While it is relatively inexpensive to keep up with fashion fads and change the look of one's wardrobe every season or so, it is a different matter when it comes to decorating our homes. Who but

the very wealthy can afford a complete decorating makeover the minute interior designers decree that minimalism is out and retro is in? Or when they dictate that ethnic artifacts are passé and the only accessories anyone with any taste should have in their home must be made from in-your-face neon pink and lime-green plastic?

In any event, many people's taste cannot be neatly pigeonholed in the way that some designers would like. Most of us find a variety of widely differing looks appealing and often cannot choose amongst them. If this describes you, then relaxed eclectic could be just what you are looking for.

Forget the confusion and clutter that often result when you try to bring together furnishings and fabrics in different styles or personal bits and pieces whose only unifying feature is the fact that you like them. In the relaxed home—where the background is simple—you can introduce whatever you please without spoiling the visual peace and sense of tranquility. Do not be worried if your bedroom ends up a mix of southern belle and geisha girl, or your living room turns into a blend of country cottage and

relaxed eclectic is a collector's dream

industrial chic, for the very purpose of relaxed eclecticism is to cross many boundaries and create unexpected combinations.

So where might you find inspiration? Your travels could well be the starting point. If you have been abroad, you are sure to have brought back some souvenirs. These are supposed to act as reminders of places we have visited, but so often, once we are home, they are put away in a drawer or cabinet, then forgotten. With relaxed eclecticism you can take them out, dust them off, and use them as the basis for some chic interior decoration. For instance, paper currency brought home from far-flung parts of the globe make an original display with photographs and other memorabilia, or pieces of ethnic fabric can be brought together on a bulletin board or in a cluster of mismatched frames.

Places you dream of but may never have visited can also spark a stream of ideas. Be inspired by the sun-drenched colors of India or Morocco, by the bold floral fabrics of Haiti, or by a collection of delicate Chinese paper lanterns.

Why buy new when retro has far more character? If you love shopping at junk shops, flea markets, and antiques stalls, do not hide your purchases away in a cupboard. The relaxed eclectic approach to decorating means that you can put your finds on show without your home ending up looking like a museum. The secret is to keep to a neutral, unifying background—understated walls and floors—so that furniture and accessories from different eras will look good together. The owner of this house has succesfully combined pieces from the fifties and sixties with modern, hand-thrown vases.

If you collect like a magpie, your collections can also be a starting point for some relaxed eclectic decoration. You may have closets full of vintage clothing, pieces of antique fabric, silk flowers, record covers, retro ceramics, modern paintings, old postcards—the possibilities are as endless as your imagination. Show these off on your mantelshelf against simple walls, on a windowsill, in plain picture frames—however seems appropriate.

And if you enjoy collecting artifacts or furniture from different eras—kitsch ornaments from the fifties or seventies furniture—mix and match them for a fresh and unusual take on collecting. Remember that with relaxed eclectic, the aim is to create not a museum-like interior, but one in which you can relax and feel comfortable. You could even go one step further and mix antique and contemporary, formal and informal, urban and rural.

left and above Furniture and accessories from the fifties have clean, simple lines that give a sense of air and space to a room. These are qualities that create the perfect environment for relaxed living. Here a classic fifties sofa on tapered wooden legs is flanked by a pair of laminate-topped Scandinavian-style side tables and two unusual lamps from the period. The floor is of polished wooden boards, and the brick wall has been painted white.

Eclecticism is so very personal that it offers the opportunity for your own special brand of humor to shine through. So indulge in delightfully whimsical displays or arrangements of objects that verge on the eccentric. Just make sure that they bring a smile to your face and stop you from taking either yourself or your sense of style too seriously. And because the look is relaxed, feel free to alter the details whenever you want, adding new treasures to a wall display, propping up a recent discovery on a shelf, replacing a collection of teacups with a row of beautiful shoes. Make an interior that is always evolving, and you will never tire of it.

However transient these eclectic decorative touches appear, remember that they are just as much a part of your decor as the paint on the walls and the floorboards. They will prove to be exactly what you need to make your relaxed home truly personal.

right, above Relaxed eclectic means surrounding yourself with things that you love. The flowing, organic form of this unique magazine rack more than earns it a place in the room.

left Allow your sense of humor free rein. Kitsch salt and pepper shakers prevent a room from becoming over-precious and taking itself too seriously.

right Unusual juxtapositions are a feature of relaxed eclectic. Here, the strictly linear sixties furniture has been given a surprising injection of feminine softness in the shape of a floral pillow cover.

relaxed
rooms

living rooms

A warmly welcoming focal point,
a generously proportioned sofa,
soothing light, and an airy feel—
these are the ingredients that will
make your living room come alive
in a truly relaxing way.

The living room usually sets the tone for the whole house. It is often the first room guests see when they come to visit, so you might feel that you have to be on your best behavior when you decorate it. But if a living room is designed to impress outsiders rather than nurture the people who live there, it will end up feeling contrived, sterile, and formal. It will certainly lack the flair and idiosyncrasy that come so easily when your guard is down and you decorate more private spaces such as bedrooms and bathrooms.

This is a shame, because the relaxed look should really come into its own in your living area; this is the place where you come to put your feet up and unwind after a long, hard day. And if you are hoping to turn your entire home into an oasis of easygoing style, the living room is a great place to start. Once you have made this space relaxed and laid-back, the rest of the house will surely follow suit.

So what is the secret of creating a relaxed living room? The first is undoubtedly to put something warm and welcoming at its heart. Too often everything in a living room revolves around the television; sofas and chairs are invariably arranged so their occupants can see the screen. The result is a space that is cold and isolating—so break the mold and choose an alternative focus.

There are plenty of possibilities. If you have the space, a fireplace makes an ideal focal point. In late fall and winter, fill it with a display of glowing logs. It can continue to be a focal point in warmer weather too; as evening falls, decorate the hearth with a cluster of gently flickering candles. Nor is there the need to feel that your fireplace has to have a conventional hearth and grate; a simple white-painted fire surround or even a plain unframed wall

left For instant nostalgia, nothing beats the chic combination of a thirties burled walnut table and great accessories such as a retro radio and an old gooseneck desk lamp. Attractive yet functional design classics like these can sometimes be found in flea markets, but they are becoming so popular that many companies are now reviving the designs and producing them for a new market. To complete—and relax—the effect, just add a few flowers in a glass.

A real log fire will always make a living area feel homey and deeply relaxed, even when the fireplace has a strictly minimal design. Intensify the coziness of the room by filling it with the warm, honey tones of wood, leather, and velvet, and by adding accessories such as a mohair and satin throw and some luxurious velvet cushions.

dancing flames in a fireplace. Try a bold, contemporary oil painting propped up on the table, a pile of sea-washed stones collected during a beachcombing expedition, an elegant foliage houseplant, or a vase of splendid fresh flowers.

When it comes to the furniture, the sofa is perhaps the most important item of all, and for the relaxed look, the more generous and indulgent its proportions, the more comfortable and inviting it will be. Position one to give the best view of a focal point,

sensuous textures
bring life to pale neutrals

opening can project just as much of a sense of warmth as an ornately carved period mantelpiece.

And if you have a mantel, resist the temptation to load it with lots of fussy ornaments. The clean lines of a vase of corkscrew willow, a few favorite framed pictures propped up on top, or a single prized artifact will have far more impact than myriad possessions.

A single particularly beautiful object placed on a side table makes another focal point that can be just as transfixing as the

far left Layer together a wealth of sensuous textures—leather, wool, velvet, and satin— to put comfort at the heart of the relaxed living room.

left and right This living room has many of the features that help create a relaxed ambience. The neutral-colored sofa is large and inviting, especially since it is covered with comfortable-looking cushions and a piece of cozy sheepskin; the large window floods the space with plenty of natural light. The airy feel of the coffee table and the simple white-painted rocking chair prevent the furniture from appearing heavy. As a bonus, the view through the window is wonderfully peaceful.

above Minimalist rooms can be cold and far from relaxed, so introduce softly muted colors for walls and furniture to counteract this tendency.

above right, right, and far right Huge windows and low, "skeletal" furniture enhance the sense of space in this modern apartment, while polished floorboards and a restrained use of textured and patterned fabrics add warmth.

for there is nothing more disconcerting than sitting facing a void. And if you have room for two sofas, so much the better. Arrange them opposite one another to create an ambience that fosters good conversation and gives the room a congenial, lived-in feel.

Daybeds or low sofas with a small back and long, welcoming seat—the traditional chaise longue—are variations on the sofa theme. They are perfect for instantly establishing a restful, slightly indolent atmosphere. Examples can be found to suit any interior, whether you are into seventies style, love the sleek lines of contemporary design, or delight in the

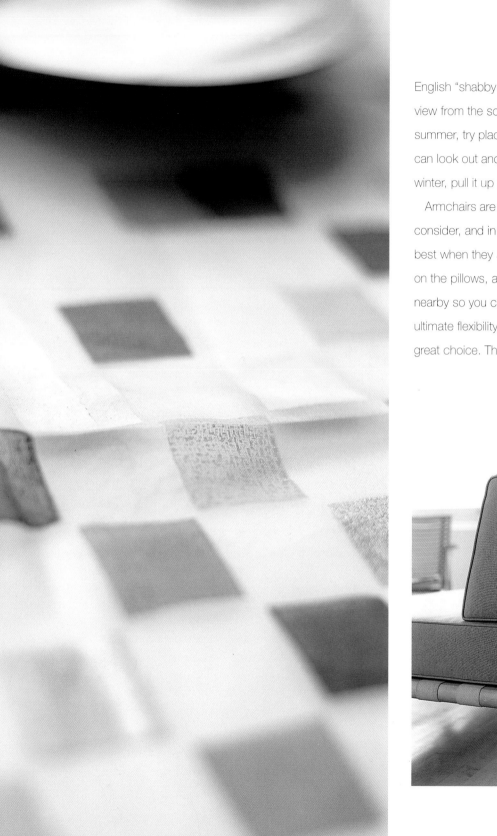

English "shabby chic" look. And the more restful the view from the sofa, the better. During spring and summer, try placing one beside a window so you can look out and enjoy the sunshine. In fall and winter, pull it up to the fireplace.

Armchairs are the next item of furniture to consider, and in the relaxed home these are at their best when they are large enough to curl up in. Pile on the pillows, and place a small stool or table nearby so you can put your feet up if you want. For ultimate flexibility and comfort, beanbag chairs are a great choice. They look stylish and certainly project

A beautiful pashmina shawl and rose-printed pillow cover bring a fresh, relaxed feel to classic sixties accessories and furniture. The juxtaposition of bright pink with the more muted retro colors is a thoroughly modern idea.

an extremely relaxed image. You will love the feeling of sinking deep into one and having it mold itself comfortably around your body; your guests will, too.

Whatever size your furniture, to ensure a sense of space and air, remember to choose as many pieces as possible on legs rather than flush with the floor. And when you are shopping for sofas and chairs, sit in them for a while—not just a moment. Many pieces are not as comfortable as they look.

As for the material you use to cover your furniture: for a timeless, sensuous effect, choose soft, pliable leather, while for an understated look, opt for simple slipcovers made from plain linen or unbleached muslin. And if pattern appeals to you, try a floral fabric—perhaps a soft-hued chintz—on a sofa or on just one occasional chair. Many people are afraid of using this traditional fabric, with its slightly old-fashioned connotations, in a contemporary context. But if you do—and especially if you keep the rest of the room pared-down and simple—it will add freshness and buzz as well as a hint of romance.

In the relaxed living room, furnishings and accessories needn't all be fitted or structured. Elegantly draped fabric or a length of material simply wound around an occasional chair will look just as

retro style with a very modern feel

above and above right
An avid collector of sixties memorabilia, the owner of this apartment has successfully created a retro mood. Shiny vinyl flooring, rough linen-effect cabinet fronts, and glass and ceramic dishes and vases give the room textural interest.

right This room, with its period window and shutters and traditional chairs, could easily have become an historical pastiche. The addition of a sixties laminate-fronted chest of drawers and an Anglepoise lamp makes for a much more relaxed approach to decorating.

left An inherently simple room is given a sense of relaxed sensuous style thanks to the funky white leather-covered beanbag, the ponyskin rug covering the floor, and the basket holding logs. The pale turquoise walls prevent any feeling of austerity from creeping in.

above and inset above Inject your own personality into a room and make it spring into life by displaying small collections of objects you find particularly appealing.

right An eclectic assortment of possessions ensures that a living room does not take itself too seriously. Formal classical touches like the plaster medallion fit surprisingly well with black denim upholstery, utilitarian lighting, sensuous fabric throws, and modern photographs.

combine the unexpected and feel free to
express your personality

good as fitted covers. You might introduce a folded woolen throw casually draped over the arm of a chair or a piece of sheepskin placed on the seat.

Because "relaxation" is the key word, you are bound to need a place to perch that cup of coffee, the novel you are reading, a vase of flowers, or the Sunday paper. Occasional tables serve the purpose, but there are other, unconventional possibilities that can establish a more effortlessly casual feel. So, try using old trunks, blanket chests, hatboxes, or wicker hampers, and place them within easy reach of your sofas and armchairs.

While most of us decorate our living rooms and position the furniture without ever thinking of changing anything until, perhaps, the next time we decorate, relaxed living means flexibility and movability—the opportunity to change a room's layout whenever we like or when we acquire something new. Introduce flexibility and movability into your living areas, and they will exude a feeling of ease and relaxed well-being. Furniture on casters is one way of achieving this effect, so try to include a couple of chairs or a small table on casters, or even a cart. Your sofa could be on casters, too.

Continue the casual theme—imagine creating the impression that you are simply passing through and may not be staying long—with pictures propped up on a mantel instead of hanging on the wall in formal

above left In a corner of a top-floor Parisian apartment a spidery utilitarian metal floor lamp meets its match in an old, spartan, rust-spotted metal chair.

above center Comfortable old red velvet armchairs are grouped with a modern cushion-scattered sofa in an arrangement that looks warmly inviting.

above right A sturdy wooden ladder increases a living room's sense of light and space as well as being an unexpected and interesting focal point in the room.

This relaxed living room capitalizes on natural colors and a wide range of textures to enhance its sense of comfort and pleasure. Heavy brown velvet floor-length draperies hang at the window, a black leather hassock sits next to a generously proportioned sofa upholstered in soft wide-wale corduroy; both are offset by a jaunty fifties chair made of cane, bamboo, and metal. The whole is enhanced by polished wooden floorboards. Inviting cushions and a mohair throw complete the effect.

left, far left, and right It is often the idiosyncratic details—a humorous printed sign, a collection of dried roots, some sensuously silky cushions—that make a room feel relaxed.

below A chaise longue is an indulgence. Underline the fact with luxurious suede cushions.

arrangements. Remember, too, that simple framed family photographs or other images you find pleasing or that have special meaning for you can decorate a room just as effectively as a piece of fine art—and such items will also add a more personal note.

Mirrors add light and sparkle to any living room, and the bigger they are, the better. In a relaxed room give them the same treatment as pictures; a huge, ornate, gilt-edged mirror, for example, might appear ostentatious hanging in the traditional position over a fireplace. For an even more relaxed—and unexpected—effect, stand it on the floor so it leans against the wall. This will be far more striking, and the temporary, makeshift image that it projects will give a

left and right This simple fireplace makes a welcoming focal point whatever the season. In warm weather, its owner fills the hearth with candles and puts fresh garden flowers on the mantelpiece. The eclectic display also includes personal mementoes collected over the years.

below and far right Calming shades of cream, off-white, and beige are used on walls and woodwork, to cover the comfortable sofa and to unify a collection of pitchers. A pair of cushions covered in vivid Chinese silk and faded English floral cotton add a burst of color and a gentle touch of romance.

sense of faded grandeur that works very comfortably with the relaxed look.

While we do not have much control over the architectural elements in our living rooms, we can make the most of those we have to ensure that they contribute to the room's sense of relaxed style. The secret is to work with, rather than against, such elements. If you adopt this approach, your living room will automatically have a sense of cohesion, since everything will be in keeping with the building as a whole.

You might, for instance, have an architectural feature such as wood paneling or a parquet floor and may feel that this is too formal for relaxed living. Not necessarily. You can make it work for you. If a relaxed simple or relaxed romantic look is what you want to achieve, or if you want a clear, neutral background for your

below and right Old luggage is easy to find (and often affordable) and makes an unusual place to stand a mirror and a plant, or rest the morning paper and a cup of tea.

right A couple of sprigs of lily of the valley in a plain wine glass combine with an unframed black and white photograph and an old rose print to make a simple, unaffected display.

possessions, then gently tone the wood down by giving it a coat of light-colored paint. Think white, gray, pale green, or cream. Alternatively, if you yearn for some warmth underfoot, you could cover your wooden floor with natural jute matting. For a more elegant but still relaxed feel, buff the wood with wax polish to reveal its textural qualities and subtle color. Darker woods such as oak and old pine have mature, rich tones and a beautiful, richly patterned grain. They make the perfect setting for one or two very special, unique pieces of classic furniture.

If you are fortunate, your living room will have large windows and be flooded with natural light. Plenty of sunshine is perhaps the greatest asset any room can have, so revel in it by avoiding fussy window treatments that will shut out the sun's rays. In fact, there is nothing to say that you need curtains or blinds at all; often, a bare window makes more of a style statement than one that is shrouded in fabric. But if your room is not private, or if you feel the need for something at the window just to soften its outline, a plain shade or delicate curtains made of voile or muslin would be the best option. Keep the look simple by avoiding valances or ornate drapery rods—curtain clips or tied tab-tops to suspend the curtains project a much more relaxed and informal image.

contemporary florals

look so fresh

left Something as simple as a down-filled, coverless quilt will soften the lines of an old, unpolished wood bench and turn it into an inviting place to relax.

right Instead of going to the trouble and expense of reupholstering chairs, try wrapping them in generous lengths of linen tied at the back. These are the quickest-to-make slipcovers you can imagine and look far less contrived than traditional upholstery.

far right Make the most of the decorative effect of your clothing and accessories. Silver shoes, left on view, have the power to make even this old staircase look elegant.

To light your relaxed living room artificially, flexibility is the key. Have several pools of lamplight or candlelight, rather than relying heavily on a central light source, and you will be able to light different corners of the room for different effects. The result will be far more soothing. Antique crystal-drop chandeliers, classic fifties Anglepoise lamps, wall sconces, and even old industrial lights will all be perfectly at home. And with relaxed living, there is no need to feel that the light fixtures all have to match one another. In fact, an eclectic mixture of styles will suit the mood better.

The colors you use on walls and ceilings will also have a bearing on the ambience you create in the living room. Good paint colors

add surprising details, then
simply relax

for a relaxed effect are neutral pale greens, beiges, grays, sky-blues and off-whites—the latter offering more warmth and softness than the minimalists' favorite pure, brilliant white.

Next, introduce splashes of brighter, more transient color in the form of pictures, lampshades, vases and bowls, throws, rugs, and pillows—feather-filled for comfort, of course—then add to the sensuous pleasure of the room by making as much use as possible of luxurious textured fabrics such as mohair, silk, velvet, or leather. Supplement these with some satin-edged blankets or fringed pashmina shawls; then, curling up on a chair or sofa or stretching out on the floor will be a luxurious experience.

Dramatic touches of black—perhaps a black denim-covered beanbag, a large black and white photograph, or a black and white pony-skin rug—can also work brilliantly in relaxed living

left This corner of a living room includes many of the ingredients of elegant living—a crystal chandelier, beautiful parquet flooring, an ornate mantel, luxurious floor-length draperies, and dramatic French windows—but they have been put together so artlessly that instead of being stiffly formal, they are the epitome of relaxed elegance.

opposite above, left and right Two very different mantelpiece arrangements show how idiosyncratic and eclectic even the smallest still life can be.

opposite below, left An enlarged photograph of roses adds a note of femininity and romance to an otherwise simply decorated wall.

opposite below, right Slipcovers, lots of soft cushions, and a woolen throw quickly give a living area an easy, relaxed feel.

rooms, provided they are used sparingly. And if your preference is for a natural, organic look, this also has a place in the relaxed living room. Just make sure that you choose accessories in natural materials such as wood, stone, leather, terra cotta, rattan, cane, rough linen, and unbleached cotton to continue the organic theme.

Finally, remember that you do not have to stand on ceremony when it comes to decorating a relaxed living room. There is as much scope for you to express your personality here as in any other part of the house. Bear in mind, too, that a living room that is truly relaxed

repose can come in many guises

Minimalism meets hippy chic in a living room that owes its relaxed charm to the innovative mix of oriental fabrics and clean, contemporary furniture. Beautiful embroidered sari fabrics and cushions made from cotton combined with leather and Chinese embroidery soften the starkness of the upholstery and make the sofa cozy and inviting. Houseplants are enjoying something of a style revival, and here they bring life and color to the huge expanse of window. The rich tones of the polished wood floor add extra warmth and texture.

does not require interior designing and careful matching of paint, accessory colors, and fabrics. If you are too intense about it, you will end up with a room that is stuffy, over-decorated, and precious, and you will have missed the point entirely.

Instead, you should just allow the room to evolve along the simplest of lines. Let it change to suit your moods, your needs,

and your lifestyle. Pick out one seriously comfortable sofa or chair, combine it with a beautiful, stylish, and sensuous object or two, and you can give a sparse, simple room all the warmth, comfort, and panache you could desire. With very little effort it will radiate an indubitably relaxed feel, and your decoration will be true to yourself as well as in harmony with the rest of your home.

kitchens
and dining rooms

An honest-to-goodness kitchen next to a simple yet stylish dining room, and everything to do with food—its preparation and eating—becomes totally relaxed.

It is often said that the kitchen is the heart of the home and should be the hub of family and social life. But the essence of the relaxed home is to allow your kitchen and dining area to meet your needs rather than your preconceptions. So although a kitchen that is cooking area, family meeting place and eating room, as well as the setting for more formal social gatherings suits some households, it may not be what you require.

If you are something of a gourmet, then you will probably want to devote a whole room of your house to dining. For many people, though, space restrictions mean that incorporating a table and chairs into the design of their kitchen is a more practical

far left Mismatched plates, collected over the years, set just the right tone for a relaxed kitchen.

left An antique panel makes an unusual backsplash, which you could easily imitate.

right and below Freestanding items in the kitchen maximize the available space and give a relaxed feel. Here, side tables and an old-fashioned refrigerator provide essential storage. The sink is the only item that cannot be moved.

formula. It is one that can work just as well for a weekday family supper as for a dinner party with friends.

When you have no choice but to put your table in the kitchen, it will have to be of the more workaday variety than a table in a separate dining room. For inevitably, the kitchen dining table will sometimes have to serve as a work surface, too. But forget the standard kitchen tables you can buy from department stores or furniture stores. A tabletop made of nothing more than bare planks resting on trestles, or an old woodworking bench, should suit the purpose admirably. Make sure that its top will withstand the heat from hot pans and plates and that it offers you a large enough surface; in your relaxed home you will almost certainly want to be paring and chopping vegetables at one end of the table while someone is writing a letter or making a shopping list at the other.

Having a large, versatile work surface such as a kitchen table in the center of your room is also part of the secret of creating a relaxed kitchen—one that is made up of freestanding pieces of furniture rather than rows of the usual built-in, made-to-measure units that have been popular for so many

above High stools and an old woodworking bench create a relaxed environment for eating. Pale cream paintwork lifts the deep tones of the furniture and the terra cotta floor.

right This room owes its character to an unusual selection of mismatched chairs and an eclectic collection of rather impressive china. The simple country table brings everything down to earth.

far right, above A beautiful collection of gilded china adds glamour to a kitchen, but its opulence is toned down by the choice of an unfussy white-painted display cabinet.

far right, below In a country-style kitchen with hints of elegant living, a vase full of casually arranged fragrant sweet peas, ensures that the sense of simple relaxed country life prevails.

there is no reason to conceal the fact that a kitchen is
a place where food is prepared and served

far left Organized chaos is the keynote of this relaxed kitchen. To emulate the look, transform a plain white refrigerator door by covering it with your favorite black and white images, then fill a wall-mounted wire basket with pots and pans. The temporary-looking kitchen sink is totally in keeping with the other elements.

left, center left, and left below Small wooden cubbyholes create valuable storage space that is also decorative. Fill each section with something different so that they all have a distinct character. The wooden frame pulls together the individual elements, but the whole looks relaxed, not over-organized.

left center Properly displayed, unusual exotic food packaging can make a decorating statement.

left For a kitchen that is the heart of a home, install an old-fashioned range and vintage cupboards.

right A kitchen with its dishes, food, and utensils on show pays tribute to its quintessential function.

years. You might also like to have a cart or mobile butcher block in the kitchen. Either of these will provide you with extra space for food preparation, somewhere to place hot pans when they come out of the oven, a spot to hang dish towels and hand towels, and perhaps a drawer for storing small gadgets and kitchen knives.

Resisting the tyranny of a kitchen with built-ins means that you cannot hide away your food, dishes, and utensils inside cabinets. This casual kitchen makes no pretense of not being a place where food is prepared: it is much more honest than its structured cousin. But do not worry that this will make it unattractive, for food and the paraphernalia of cooking can be decorative and highly appealing.

Put utensils, dishes, and groceries boldly on show on open shelves, in cubbyholes, on stainless-steel shelving; hang them from hooks or display them inside glass-fronted cabinets. Add glass jars filled with spices, bottles of oil and vinegar, packages of flour

and sugar, containers to hold wooden spoons and spatulas, and stacks of gleaming cast-iron or copper pans.

Using lots of wood in the kitchen also helps to convey a sense of honesty and relaxation. With its many natural tones and textures, wood always has a restful effect, and most other materials and colors look good with it too. So you might put a solid ash worktop next to cream-painted cabinets

next to a navy laminate or stainless-steel backsplash—all to stunning effect. No matter that the materials do not match. The result is highly practical and very relaxed.

The desire for kitchens with freestanding elements has brought a renewed interest in the look of kitchen appliances. For many years they were hidden away behind cabinet doors and decor panels. Their design became streamlined and coordinating—but sometimes a bit dull. Now, though, there is a demand for the designs of the past—butler's sinks with brass faucets, old-fashioned refrigerators with curved casings and big chrome handles, food mixers with the distinctive retro look of the thirties and—that old rural favorite—the cast-iron kitchen range. Kitchen appliances have once again become focal points, rather than something to hide away.

above left Be eclectic and shop around for fixtures with originality. These old brass faucets perfectly complement an old-fashioned sink.

above Building a kitchen from recycled lumber gives it instant character, and a collection of favorite photographs adds individuality.

But the streamlined look has its adherents and has undergone its own revolution. The result? Industrial chic, with kitchen appliances encased in chrome, stainless steel, or brushed aluminum. Dishwashers, ovens, and washing machines have even become designer pieces in their own right. And so the wheel has turned full circle: these modern appliances, like their traditional counterparts, are seen and admired instead of being hidden away. Today's streamlined kitchens have a far more honest feel than the streamlined kitchens that were fashionable twenty years ago.

right Dining thirties-style does not have to feel as formal as in those days. A nice relaxed touch is to cover the dining table only partway, allowing the warm, honey tones of the wood to be appreciated. And instead of sticking strictly to period accessories, this collector has hung a stunning pair of working drawings by the contemporary English sculptor Alan Grimwood on the walls.

below right This battered old tea tin and candles in a hand-carved wooden bowl could have been hidden away in a cabinet, but instead they have become a decorative still life.

the natural tones of wood are restful and timeless

But whether you choose to buy designer appliances encased in industrial-chic metal or traditionally styled models with a nostalgic retro feel, you must be prepared to spend a little more on them than you would on conventional items. It is all a case of juggling priorities. If you are not going to pay to hide appliances behind cabinets, you would instead do well to spend your money on acquiring well designed kitchen basics that are truly worthy of being on view.

As a background to kitchen appliances, it is best to keep the colors of the kitchen muted. Lots of white is always a winner and cannot fail to look clean and crisp, but a few soft pale colors can add a touch of

opposite, left Relaxed kitchens do not have to be furnished with made-for-kitchen furniture. Here, an industrial steel bench is reinvented as an extra worktop in the kitchen.

opposite, right Create an utterly simple, totally relaxed decoration by stringing together some favorite objects and hanging them on a plain white wall.

above A simple kitchen display is nothing more than a row of silver mugs and a dangling scoop.

left The monastic feel of a dining room is softened by swathes of antique white linen and the abundance of light entering through elegant French windows.

charm. However, if your kitchen tends to be the hub of all activity in your household, a uniform color scheme will help to unify the space and make it feel more peaceful.

The more neutral the decor, the fewer the restrictions when it comes to choosing dishes and glassware. In the relaxed kitchen,

elegant yet unfussy dining and
a sunny kitchen sink

slavish style and color-coordination are a thing of the past. A mix-and-match approach will give the room a more carefree feel. Try sturdy glass or plastic tumblers alongside ornate gold-decorated porcelain, secondhand flowery plates from a flea market or wooden

opposite Relaxed elegance is the main player in this dining room. Although on a large scale, the furniture is simple. Painting it to blend with the walls and woodwork removes any tendency toward excessive formality and helps to unify the space.

left and right, above and below Displays of vibrant ceramics and flatware can be changed whenever you feel like it.

above Why not feel cheerful while you are washing the dishes? Canary yellow tiles bring some sunshine and a sense of fun to a small kitchen, showing how color can transform even the most restricted space.

bowls brought back from a tropical vacation
next to plain pure white china, chunky hand-
thrown pots and plates alongside delicate
Moroccan tea glasses. Forget purism. Once
you have a relaxed kitchen, when you see a
piece of glassware or a plate that you
absolutely must have, you can buy it without
worrying whether or not it will match.

When it comes to relaxed homes with the
space for a separate dining room, there is
even more scope for your imagination. For if
you are lucky enough to have one, a
separate dining room is where relaxed
elegance can truly come into its own. Think
generously sized tables, crisp tablecloths,
and ornate chairs. And, as in the
kitchen/dining room, in the relaxed dining

room there is no need to worry whether or not your accessories match. If anything, mismatched china, glassware, and flatware will help to create an easier-going atmosphere, and you will feel more inclined to use the dining room on a regular basis. Airy, neutral walls and floors, fine linen, an old candelabra, and an eclectic assortment of glassware and patterned china—all these will defuse any tendency toward excessive formality while still imparting glamour on special occasions.

Whether you have a separate dining room or a kitchen/dining room, remember that you are more likely to focus on the delicious food and the company of family or friends if your surroundings are simple, stylish, and thoroughly relaxed. Whether you're dining alone or with others, everything about the room should encourage you just to kick your shoes off under the table, eat your fill, and enjoy.

left and far left Pale woods and white laminate prevail in this dining room, but eating there could be a rather sterile experience. Introduce a hint of nature for a relaxing touch—a display of full-blown hydrangeas in a galvanized vase and a contemporary piece of artwork consisting of individual ceramic panels united by their warm, natural earth colors.

above Only with an eye for the relaxed eclectic look would one have the courage to combine the warm honey tones of an Art Deco dining set with an industrial-style stainless-steel kitchen.

right A collection of unusual glass and ceramics displayed on an unconventional shelf unit adds a personal note to a minimalist kitchen/dining area.

bedrooms

A relaxed bedroom is whatever you want it to be, so pamper yourself with soothing colors, luxurious bedding, your own special books, magazines, and photographs, and an unashamedly special bed.

Just a few touches are all you need to make a pared-down space gently romantic. A lofty all-white room with old utilitarian metal lockers standing against one wall can be given just a hint of relaxed romance with understated floral pillowcases and a beautiful filmy throw, or perhaps with a sheer, floral curtain. A four-poster bed and a bunch of flowers are other subtle romantic touches. The galvanized steel scaffolding poles of the bed and the severe, industrial bucket holding the flowers prevent bed and flowers from being overly sentimental.

A bedroom is the most private space in the home, the one room you should be able to decorate as you like and fill with whatever makes you feel relaxed, happy, and cosseted. For maximum relaxation, this usually means giving the bedroom a rather traditional ambience, using furniture that is familiar rather than innovative, bedding that is luxurious rather than spartan, colors that are soothing rather than invigorating.

A bedroom offers no shortage of opportunity to use a wealth of super-soft blankets, duvets, pillows, bolsters, quilts, and eiderdowns. Do not stint on these—the more you put together and the more layered the finished effect, the more powerful the sense of ease and softness will be. During the colder months, put wool and mohair blankets on top of heavy feather-filled quilts, piling them all up on the bed in generous folds. Then, when the weather warms up, swap them for crisp cotton sheets and subtly embroidered pillowcases, layered with light bedcovers and throws.

Complement this layered look by using plenty of fabrics elsewhere in the room, too. Fabrics at the window will help to cocoon you. Pick sheers in hot pinks and reds to cast a warm glow and make the space feel comfortable and sheltering. Add a selection of contrasting fabrics for upholstery, pillows, or bedspreads, and you will find yourself with some wonderful juxtapositions that can give the room unparalleled depth. You might end up with

full of lightness and dreams

left and below An ornately carved antique four-poster bed has been painted white to blend with the white-painted brickwork of the walls. Against this pared-down background, an eclectic collection of Asian fabrics and rose-sprigged pillowcases, found in a flea market, add an injection of relaxing, welcome color.

a gold-embroidered sari used as an exotic throw on top of a mohair blanket; you could admire a fragile-looking floral pillowcase alongside a boldly printed rayon dress; you could place a beanbag covered in ethnic ikat beside a pile of old army blankets; you could drape a traditional patchwork quilt over a batik sheet. Indulge your fancy, for this is relaxed eclecticism at its best.

And instead of hanging all your clothing inside closets, add to the visual feast by placing favorite garments—anything from denim jackets and cocktail dresses to cotton sheaths and cashmere cardigans—on pretty fabric-covered hangers and displaying them against a wall, suspended from the frame of a mirror, on a hook behind the door, or just draped over the arm of a chair.

gorgeous beds take center stage in simple surroundings

left In another simple bedroom, the bed area is once again the room's welcoming focal point. In this case, an understated, completely plain double bed is brought to life with a huge painting by the American artist Peter Zangrillo substituting for a headboard. An old patchwork quilt covering the bed stands in sharp contrast to the painting, bringing together old and new strands of America's artistic heritage and adding a feeling of homey comfort. In true relaxed style, a couple of old trunks stand by the bed in place of a bedside table. For those of us not fortunate enough to possess a work of art, a beautiful length of fabric, or an alluring piece of vintage clothing could take pride of place over a bed in the same way.

left Make diary entries in the privacy of your bedroom. Delicate flower-embroidered sheets make a complementary background for a journal covered in a bold, geometric-print fabric.

right above and below Why hide away lovely ethnic jewelry or fabrics bought in an oriental bazaar? In a relaxed bedroom, Indian glass bangles can grace a bed post, and a bolt of Chinese silk makes an eye-catching splash of color on a chair. All this goes to show that in a relaxed bedroom, the supporting cast is as important as the principal actors.

far right Delicately embroidered sheets and pillowcases, a gauzy pink curtain, and a pair of Chinese silk slippers make a plain bedroom into an oasis of calm femininity, where rest and relaxation prevail.

If you are short of closet space, you can simply hang your clothing on hooks, so that it becomes part of the decor. But for open-plan storage such as this, bear in mind that sturdy wooden coat hangers are better looking than wire or plastic hangers, and make sure that your clothes are neat and clean. And if you add a collection of beaded evening bags, some pieces of antique lace, or a rack of strappy sequined sandals to your bedroom display, the effect will be even more distinctive and personal.

A collection of sixties furniture forms the basis for the decoration of this New York apartment. The dark wood and laminate bedside table holds an unusual retro telephone and an angular fifties metal lamp. The table stands on an austere pedestal on rubber feet. To prevent the room from looking like a museum piece, the owner has used an eye-catching piece of handblocked floral fabric as a throw on the bed.

Hiding beneath these richly built-up layers of clothing, bedding, and accessories, the bedroom furniture you choose definitely must include an unabashedly striking bed—perhaps a sybaritic four-poster in traditional or contemporary style, a nostalgic antique wrought-iron or showy brass bed, a bed constructed from starkly plain industrial scaffolding, an elegant sleigh bed, or a minimalist futon. Any one of these would make an imposing focal point, and even a futon or a low-lying Hollywood bed would lack nothing in terms of comfort if you were to place it against plain walls and deck it out in the simplest white bed linen. In fact, with the right choice of good-looking sheets and coverings, even a mattress on the floor could become the perfect bed.

Mirrors are another essential, increasing the amount of light and giving the room a dreamlike quality. You will certainly want a small mirror for putting on makeup, but when it comes to seeing yourself full length, choose the largest mirror you can find and give it the relaxed treatment by standing it on the floor rather than hanging it

on the wall or hiding it away on the inside of a closet door. For a touch of glamour, choose a mirror with an ornately carved natural or gilded wood frame: for a simpler effect, keep the mirror as plain as plain can be. Either way, you will want it on display.

Maintain the sense of light and space by keeping your color scheme simple and based on pastel colors, using sky-blues, powder-pinks, gentle lilacs, pale turquoises, and white. Window

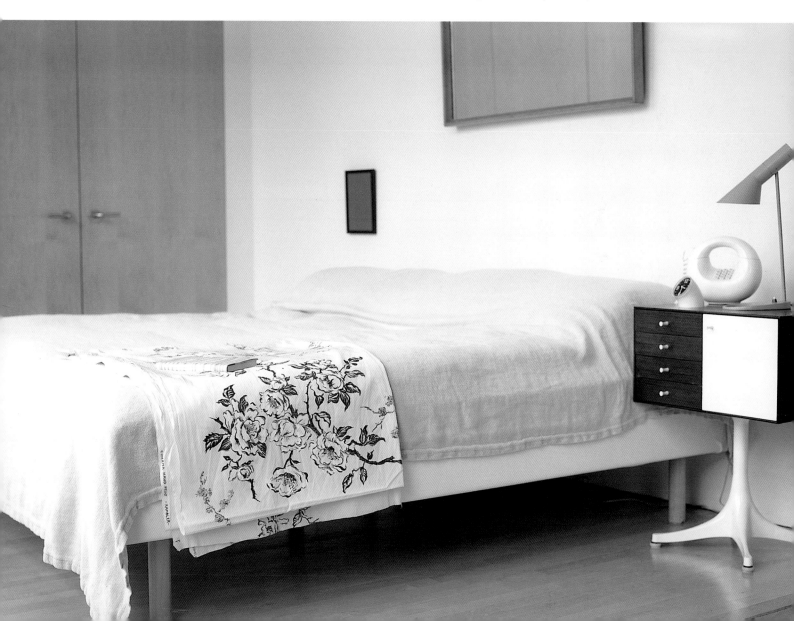

far left and below A soft honeycomb-weave throw adds a flash of bright color and a sense of coziness to a masculine, almost monastic, room.

right Even a small collection of eclectic retro pieces on a mantel can be a conversation point.

far right The owners of this thirties apartment have taken the style of the building as the starting point for their interior decoration. Venetian blinds and a sturdy glass-fronted bookcase suit its mood, but the modern vases and cardboard-covered drum add hints of individuality.

treatments should be as minimalist as possible. Avoid heavy draperies and if your bedroom is open to view, consider Venetian blinds or muslin panels. These strike just the right balance between providing privacy and allowing daylight in.

Add the rest of your bedroom furnishings according to your needs and the available space. Instead of confining yourself to a dressing table and chest of drawers, it is more original—and very relaxed—to borrow from other parts of the house. Import a favorite armchair from your living room to provide you with a comfortable place to sit and read a book in peace at any time of the day. Steal a pretty chair from the dining room to use as

fill your bedroom with whatever makes you happy

a bedside table. Coat racks, usually seen exclusively in hallways, make perfect makeshift closets, while old school lockers, more often filled with junk and standing dully in a utility room, will provide extra, unconventional storage space. Prop up a large oil painting behind a Hollywood bed in place of a headboard. Use open shelf units from the kitchen to display your shoes and bags. Hang jewelry from old dressmaker's dummies, string it around decorative lampshades, or pile it high in pretty china dishes. Fill a shopping basket with scarves and gloves and stand it on the floor or on a small table.

The secret is to remember that a bedroom does not have to be only a bedroom. If you blur the boundaries a little, it can become part-boudoir, part-dressing room, part-private living room. Collections of books, magazines, paintings, plants, and

opposite and above right
There is no better room to turn into a haven of sensousness than the bedroom. Here wood, cane, crisp bed linens, straw baskets, antique lace and embroidery, and gold-encrusted Indian shawls combine in an easy-spirited way.

left and above For glamour and elegance, drape a sheer, gold-trimmed sari over an old sofa.

right Secondhand store furnishings make an unusual choice for bedroom storage.

left Make a cool bedroom feel welcoming with a sumptuous, velvet-trimmed bedspread.

below left and below Revel in the unusual juxtaposition of a utilitarian desk lamp and a seventies light fixture with a completely over-the-top carved wooden bed. These are the sort of surprising combinations that relaxed eclectic makes possible.

opposite You can easily personalize an all-white bedroom simply by clipping family photographs around the room on lengths of thin wire. Beautiful turquoise bed linen adds color, warmth, and romance.

photographs find a home where once there were just clothes and toiletries. Include piles of paperbacks here and there, line shelves with framed snapshots, hang your favorite artwork on walls and decorate windowsills with anything from rows of pretty glass perfume bottles to pots of colorful geraniums. Add vases of simply arranged fresh flowers, too, as a delicate counterpoint to all the other precious possessions in the room.

Implement just a few of these ideas, and you will create the perfect relaxed bedroom, somewhere you will want to linger during daylight hours instead of only retreating to at night.

bathrooms

Defy convention. The relaxed
bathroom can be as romantic,
glamorous, minimalist, or retro
as you choose. Just add the
personal touches you love
most, then lie back and
indulge yourself.

left Old-fashioned chrome faucets and an unusual plug device give this plain white bathroom sink antique charm.

below and right This bathroom captures the spirit of times past and the beauty to be found in utility. The star is the freestanding, rolltop bathtub. The shelf unit, bathroom scale, and wooden bench convey a similar effect.

Decorating your bathroom gives you the chance to create a haven of relaxation, a place where you can just soak away your stresses and strains. But to make the room as therapeutic as possible—and to maintain the spirit of relaxed living—you need to include some deeply personal touches. Only you can know which details will help you unwind and feel at ease, so close your eyes and imagine your ideal, absolutely restful bathroom.

If the image you conjure up is one of femininity and glamour, you should have some floral patterns and soft fabrics in your bathroom alongside the usual fixtures. Warm up the ubiquitous white of the room with colors such as strong, hot pinks or

vivacious turquoises. Let everyone know how much you love life's pleasures by lining your bathroom shelves with your favorite toiletries and cosmetics displayed in old glass bottles and jars or in a selection of bowls and baskets.

Alternatively, your perfect bathroom might be altogether simpler, possibly even verging on the austere and monastic. This is a place where there is nothing to distract you from the ritual of cleansing mind and body. Wetrooms—essentially open-plan, completely waterproofed spaces—are the simplest bathrooms of all. For these you need a floor that slopes gently so the water can drain away, waterproof walls, a powerful shower, and some basic, functional accessories such as big blocks of soap, natural sponges, and loofahs. Then just add a simple wooden seat or stool and a row of plain wooden pegs to hang up your bath towels.

Some people find that a sleek modern bathroom is what they need to feel at ease. These bathrooms make the most of materials such as concrete, glass, and

use gauzy curtains for a
touch of glamour

far left and left Create a retro-style bathroom with brick-shaped tiles, an old shower fitting and accessories such as this bathroom scale from a flea market.

below Crisp linen towels are piled on an old dentist's cabinet, which now serves as bathroom storage.

opposite Sheer beaded curtains bring color and glamour to a monochromatic bathroom and contrast with the utilitarian fixtures.

stainless steel; they have an almost industrial feel to them. If this is the look that appeals to you, choose features such as stainless steel or stone sinks, chrome designer faucets or sandblasted glass shower screens. The plainer the details, the better, but to make the effect just a little softer and more relaxed, try adding a pile of fluffy towels, or a single flower in a glass vase.

Alternatively, you may long to create a bathroom with a retro feel, using reclaimed fixtures that are authentic to a particular time. Old tiles, metal-framed bathroom shelves, ornate, solidly made faucets and shower heads, thick chrome towel rails, an old-fashioned bathroom scale—all give a sense of the bath-times enjoyed by the comfortable middle class a hundred or so years ago.

above Although this bathroom has a sense of the past, it is not a museum piece. Painting the walls blue, the outside of the tub black, and the woodwork and floor white brings it up to date. The textured cotton rug adds some softness.

above right An alcove makes an attractive bathroom display area. Matching chrome-lidded storage jars hold bathroom necessities, while the brown tones of a seashell collection complement a bowl of wooden-handled toothbrushes.

In a retro bathroom, aim to give the space the sort of honesty that is so often lacking in modern bathrooms where everything is hidden away behind panels or inside built-in units. Achieve this freer look by following the principle that there is beauty in utility—in other words, revel in the bold designs of the hardware of the past. You could start by installing a big freestanding cast-iron, rolltop bathtub in pride of place in the center of the room. Or indulge

side, so if you are used to bathing in a cramped tub, or using a tiny sink, you will find the older versions extremely practical. Nothing is more relaxing than to be able to stretch out in a deep turn-of-the-century bathtub. What is more, you can personalize your bathtub by painting its exterior—black for impact, white for simplicity, cream for classic restraint. The feet of the tub can also tell a story: choose ball-and-claw feet for total authenticity or streamlined chrome for a more unexpected combination.

As with the relaxed bedroom, there is no reason why your bathroom should not borrow pieces of furniture or accessories

plain and simple backdrops,
attention to detail

from other rooms in the house—perhaps an armchair or a decorative rug from the living room, an ornate serving cart or chair from the dining room, a painted wooden chest of drawers from the bedroom, a coat rack from the hall. Any of these additions would lend a relaxed, uniquely personal character to your bathroom and will prevent it from looking as if it has just emerged from the sterile, lifeless pages of some impersonal catalog.

yourself with an old-fashioned telephone-type shower. You might even find the courage to leave your bathroom's pipework on display instead of concealing it.

Do not worry that this honest, practical approach will mean that you have to sacrifice comfort. In the early days of indoor plumbing, bathrooms were, by modern standards, huge. This meant that bathtubs and sinks were also on the generous

above left and left All-white walls and ceiling form the background for this small Parisian bathroom—which is actually a wetroom. Dispensing with the usual shower screen means that there is greater flexibility in the use of the space. The floor, sloping gently toward a drain in the center of the room and covered with bold blue and beige tiles, is the focal point.

119

A hint of wood, some pale ocher-
colored tiles, a few fluffy towels, and
some bottles and jars, just visible
through a frosted glass panel, make
a stark bathroom feel more welcoming.

soft fluffy towels and favorite photographs
meet minimalism

For the floor, simple flooring looks best and is most practical. Bare floorboards are easy to clean; you can make them more user-friendly with the addition of a plain white cotton rug here and there. The modern bathroom needs something more refined underfoot— perhaps marble or terrazzo—while for the industrial-looking bathroom, concrete flooring is preferred. Linoleum is back in fashion and is once again being manufactured in a wide range of colors and designs. It is the perfect choice for retro bathrooms. Another flooring option comes in the form of ceramic tiles, which can be used to create any number of special effects, from the subtle decorative qualities of encaustic insets to the clean, clinical look of glazed tiles in purest, plainest white.

If you want to give an existing bathroom a relaxed makeover, there are many simple ways of doing it. Try covering the walls with

far left and left If you are the sort of person who regards getting clean as something to be done as quickly and efficiently as possible, then this must be the bathroom of your dreams. With its concrete walls and floor and steel countertop and sink unit, it exudes a sense of cool competence, tempered only by the presence of a single photograph.

With plain white walls and an unfinished concrete floor as a starting point, the owner of this bathroom could easily have taken its decoration in the direction of minimalism. Instead, the simple background has been given an injection of romance and femininity. The effect is fresh and utterly charming and has been achieved merely by the use of a single rose-printed cotton curtain gently filtering the light from the large window, and a single glassful of flowers. The sense of light is magnified by the large thirties mirror over the sink, while the freestanding rolltop bathtub adds a leisured feel. A white-painted cabinet is another light touch.

industrial chic
and delicate florals
create an air of romance

tongue-and-groove paneling painted in white or gently muted pink, blue or green to ensure that the room feels spacious and airy. Glass shelves are perfect, too. Besides bringing a sense of light to a bathroom, they provide valuable and practical storage space. And instead of a dull, standard bathroom mirror, try finding an old mirror. It does not need to have a beautiful gilded antique frame, or a spectacular Venetian glass frame—although these would, of course, be lovely. Any unusual, old, well-proportioned mirror will catch the eye and make your bathroom a little bit different.

In a similar vein, an antique washstand makes a lovely perch for a pile of towels, some natural sponges, and other bath-time treats. And instead of putting your soap in a standard soap dish, try the more relaxed effect of using a favorite china bowl, perhaps one large enough to hold several soaps from which you can choose according to your mood. And finally, do not forget flowers. The bathroom is one room we often forget to decorate with flowers, but a small, simple arrangement will go a long way toward creating an atmosphere that verges tantalizingly on the sybaritic.

It can be as simple as this to make a relaxed, truly personal bathroom that is as glamorous and distinctive as the rest of your home. Most of the work has been done for you, for many of the good things in life—plenty of hot running water, piles of soft towels, and your favorite toiletries—are probably already in place. The rest is only a short step away.

workrooms

A comfortable workspace means a creative worker, so make your home office relaxing, turn your back on standard-issue office furniture, and feed your senses while you work.

More and more people are choosing to work from home instead of commuting to an impersonal office every day. But even if you are not a full-time home-worker, you probably still need a home workstation, somewhere to deal with household accounts and office work brought home, to pay bills and write letters. Use some of the following simple ideas, and there is no reason why this space should not be as relaxed and stylish as the rest of your home.

The first rule is, get personal. To maximize your creativity, you need to be comfortable and surrounded by some of your favorite things. No one is at his or her best working in cramped conditions and surrounded by bland walls and anonymous office equipment. So instead of a mass-produced office desk, start with a simple trestle table, an old-fashioned writing desk, or a pine dining table.

sugared-almond
colors defy convention

Next, you need a comfortable chair that is ergonomically suited to the work you do. Instead of a standard-issue office chair, choose one you really like—perhaps a Charles Eames design classic, a padded dining chair, or an antique office clerk's chair. If you like, dress it up with a new cover, and to add a sense of fun and irreverence, choose an unusual material, one not usually seen in a work environment—fake fur, faded chintz, jazzy vinyl, or raw linen.

A touch of humor will also help make your room feel less like a conventional workspace. Use a dressmaker's dummy to pin notes on, or make a bulletin board for things that will inspire you as you

opposite, above An ingenious cabinet doubles as desk and office storage. Close the doors at the end of the day and relax.

opposite, below Be carried far away from the world of work with a desk made from a white-painted pasting table and unexpected, lilac-painted walls.

right, top left An alcove with shelves makes an ideal place to store binders or box files.

right, top right Sometimes there is no point in disguising the fact that offices are about work, but with careful planning you can arrange the tools of your trade so they are aesthetically pleasing.

right, below left Make sure you surround yourself with good-looking office equipment like these notebooks and paperweight.

right, below right Organization is the key to office spaces that really work well, and systematically color-coordinating your paperwork can be half the battle. These matching box files also create blocks of color that help to unify the space.

work—postcards, magazine clippings, fabric swatches, photos.

Once you have stamped your personality on your workroom, you need a degree of order and discipline to make it work well and to ensure that your stress levels do not escalate as you struggle to locate a file or find a document. So some sort of filing system is essential, but why be conventional?

Shoe boxes covered in pretty fabrics or old hatboxes or trunks can provide the organization you need and are attractive. You could try color-coordinating the smaller elements—blue for household bills, yellow for professional accounts, and so on.

left   The home office for the person who likes clarity of thought. A polished concrete floor and blank walls are brought to life with a no-nonsense red leather chair.

right above and opposite A fashion designer who works from home finds inspiration in a wall covered from top to bottom with magazine and newspaper clippings, fabric swatches—even plastic bags and soap packaging.

right center and below Even if your taste in office decoration veers toward the minimalist, you can loosen up and relax a little by adding a couple of roses in a glass to a shelf full of useful books.

who says work cannot be creative?

left A modern chair contrasts with an old
scrubbed-pine table in an office where you can
stay cool, calm, and collected whatever your
schedule. Work is stored beneath the desk in
boxes draped casually with linen towels, while
candles on the table add a personal touch.

below Keep some much-loved possessions
nearby to remind you of life beyond work.

right A sense of unity is maintained in this busy
home workspace by sticking to a simple scheme
of white and natural wood.

Other low-tech storage, such as a selection of old cans in place of standard plastic pen holders, makes a humorous contrast with the fax machine, phone, and computer. With touches such as these, there is never the risk that the room will be overtaken by soulless plastic.

If you cannot dedicate a whole room to your office but have to work in a corner of another room, you might consider a large armoire combining desk and storage space. Alternatively, hunt out an old, all-concealing rolltop desk, or screen off the area with an attractive room divider.

Whatever kind of workspace you need, get the balance right between discipline and freedom, and any work you do will seem much more enjoyable.

far left A velvet-covered seat turns a utilitarian tubular metal chair into a relaxing place to sit; home office furniture does not have to be ordinary.

center left A desk lamp for good directional light is essential. Never mind that the desk is fifty years older than the lamp: the two still look stylish together.

left Do away with conventional office storage. This wire basket is just the right size to hold computer floppy disks.

above, left and right Decorate your workspace with images of friends and family and with favorite treasures.

right Influences from different places and eras make a home office area that is totally relaxed. Here a pierced metal lamp from North Africa stands near a retro desk lamp and a more modern phone, clock, and photographs.

outdoors

Combine beautiful plants and
easygoing furniture in relaxed
outdoor spaces, then feel
the healing power of nature
and counteract the stress.

relaxed rooms

In today's hi-tech world, people live life at a hectic pace. To relax, many of us need to reestablish some link, however small, with nature. By creating an outdoor room or other space that blurs the boundaries between outside and in, you can benefit from the healing powers of nature without even leaving the confines of your home.

You do not need to have a large garden to achieve this. Your outdoor room could just as easily be a sunroom, the tiniest backyard, a sunny verandah, a lean-to shed, a shady porch, or simply a room with large French windows. If you are really short of space, your

left Never mind that you have only a porch as your outdoor space. Be relaxed about it, take a huge, comfortable chair from the living room whenever the sun shines, sit back, and enjoy.

right You do not need special furniture for a relaxed outdoor space. A simple folding chair makes a perfect perch for pots filled with summer plants.

far right Place a simple wooden bench on a wide verandah so you can sit outside whenever you feel the urge. All you need add in order to feel completely relaxed is a soft flower-covered cushion.

link with nature need be nothing more than a collection of window boxes or some flowerpots by the front door.

To give your outdoor room the same unique style as the rest of your house, treat it just as you would any other room. Make it relaxed and natural, and remember to choose furniture and accessories that you really love. To start with, you do not need to buy expensive new garden furniture. One of the delights of relaxed

137

living is to discover that modestly priced rattan furniture and junk-shop finds are even more at home outdoors than in. If you can find them, pieces such as daybeds and deck chairs will always add a relaxed, languorous air, but if there is no room to keep more than a tiny, old rickety garden chair outdoors, then do not worry. When the weather turns fine, simply take a small, comfortable armchair and some soft, squishy cushions from the living room, sit, and enjoy.

Roughly finished wooden furniture is another excellent choice for your outdoor room. Its earthiness will help you feel more in touch with nature. Accessorize with plenty of terra cotta pots, basketware, ethnic textiles and, for indoor/outdoor spaces, unvarnished wood floors. Or, if you prefer more elegance, masses of exotic plants accompanied by dark wood furniture and swathes of sheer fabric, mosquito-net style, add tropical grandeur.

Sensuosness plays a large part in the enjoyment of any outdoor space. Revel in the sight and texture of your plants, whether a collection of luscious houseplants, troughs of flowering annuals, or a selection of evergreens. Scented plants add another dimension to one's enjoyment, especially in sunrooms where the warmth heightens their fragrance. And if a sunroom is out of the question, fill a room with intoxicating scent by planting a honeysuckle or jasmine outside a window, or by putting some aromatic herbs in a window box on the windowsill.

Besides enjoying these sights and smells, you will find that tending your plants is a fantastic stress-buster. And caring for your outdoor space will give you an outlet for your nurturing and creative skills, as well as being a constructive way to spend your time. If your outdoor room is as relaxed as the rest of your house, nothing will be able to spoil your tranquillity.

far left and far right Give foliage houseplants the relaxed treatment with a huge gilt mirror propped up among them and some exotic accessories.

left What could look more relaxed than these fifties cane chairs set in a tiny wood-floored roof garden against a wall of terra cotta tiles?

right above If outdoor space is at a premium, simply open the door and relax in an old wrought iron chair with potted plants on the floor. A delicate chandelier adds a charming and elegant touch.

right The deck chair comes up to date to provide the ultimate in sophisticated relaxation.

suppliers

Anthropologie
375 West Broadway
New York, NY 10012
call 800 309 2500 for store locations
Quirky furniture and home furnishings.

Atlantic Blanket Company
135 North Road
Swans Island, ME 04685
888 526 9526
www.AtlanticBlanket.com
Soft, hand-woven wool blankets in
solids, stripes, and checks; mail order.

Bed, Bath & Beyond
call 800 GOBEYOND for store
locations
www.bedbath&beyond.com
Chain of more than 200 stores selling
contemporary home accessories.

B&J Fabrics
263 W. 40th Street
New York, NY 10018
212 354 8150
Cotton and silk fabrics; mail order.

Calvin Klein Home
call 800 294 7978 for store locations
Bed and bath linens and accessories.

Circle Fabrics
263 W. 38th Street
New York, NY 10018
212 719 5153
Range of decorator fabrics, including
raffia and colored canvas.

The Company Store
800 323 8000
www.the companystore.com
West Coast chain and mail-order
supplier of mattresses, pillows,
cotton bed linens; mail order.

Country Curtains
800 876 6123
www.countrycurtains.com
Traditional curtains; mail order.

Crate & Barrel
call 800 996 9960 for store locations
www.crateandbarrel.com
Contemporary furnishings, furniture,
linens, and glassware; mail order.

Cuddledown of Maine
312 Canco Road
Portland, ME 04103
800 323 6793 or 207 865 1713
www.cuddledown.com
Bed linens, including European
down comforters; mail order.

Denyse Schmidt Quilts
68 Riverside Drive
Fairfield, CT 06430
800 621 9017
Offbeat reinterpretations of traditional
American patchwork; mail order.

Calvin Klein Home

Elizabeth Eakins Inc.
21 E. 65th Street
New York, NY 10021
212 628 1950
Handwoven rugs in wool, cotton,
and linen; wide variety of patterns.

Fran Jay's Glassware
P. O. Box 10
Lambertville, NJ 08530
609 397 1571
www.glassshow.com
All kinds of old glass kitchenware,
including Pyrex and Depression glass;
mail order only.

Fran's Wicker and Rattan Furniture
Dept. 126, 295 Route 10
Succasunna, NJ 07876
888 999 2629 or 973 584 2230
www.franswicker.com
Offers a wide range of wicker and
rattan furniture in many styles for
indoors and outdoors; mail order.

Garnet Hill
800 622 6216
Contemporary furnishings and
furniture, including design classics;
mail order only.

Home Depot
call 800 553 3199 for store locations
www.homedepot.com
Lighting, kitchen cabinets, and
bathroom fixtures.

Indigo Seas
123 N. Robertson Blvd.
Los Angeles, CA 90048
310 550 8758
Treasure-house of furnishings from
Western Europe, Morocco, and India
with a nostalgic, exotic flavor.

Ironworks
165 Waterman Drive
South Portland, ME 04106
207 799 1185
Hand-forged wrought-iron lamps,
lighting fixtures, and accessories;
mail order.

Irreplaceable Artifacts
14 Second Ave.
New York, NY 10003
212 777 2900
www.irreplaceableartifacts.com
Salvaged light fixtures and
antique plumbing.

Lancaster County, Pennsylvania
For Amish quilts—the area contains
dozens of stores selling these
American classics.

The Lively Set
33 Bedford Street
New York, NY 10014
212 807 8417
Antique American furnishings, mainly
from the Twenties to the Fifties.

Lucullus
610 Chartres Street
New Orleans, LA 70130
504 528 9620
Great range of antiques relating to
gastronomy—furniture, silverware,
glass,and kitchenware.

**Metro Shelving/
George Burke Com.**
1563 FDR Station
New York, NY 10150
212 888 6393
Modular system of industrial steel
furniture, custom-designed to order.

New York Central Art Supply
62 Third Avenue
New York, NY 10003
212 473 7705
Silk for painting on; mail order.

Palais Royal
1725 Broadway Street
Charlottesville, VA 22902
call 804 979 3911 for store locations
www.palais.com
East Coast chain offering imported
French bed and bath linens; mail order.

Past Present Future
336 East Franklin Avenue
Minneapolis, MN 55404
call 800 801 2523 or 323 852 7120
Restored metal office furniture; mail order.

Pottery Barn
P. O. Box 7044
San Francisco
CA 94120-7044
call 800 922 9934 for store locations
www.potterybarn.com
Furniture and decorative details, such
as curtains, china, and pillows.

Real Goods Catalog
800 762 7325
www.realgoods.com
West Coast chain offering ecologically
friendly home accessories, many made
from recycled materials; mail order.

Rejuvenation Lamp & Fixture Co.
888 343 8548
www.rejuvenation.com
Reproductions of antique light fixtures;
mail order.

Renninger's Antique and
Collectors' Market
740 Noble Street

Kutztown, PA 19530
610 683 6848
www.renningers.com
Big, 1,400-booth flea markets are
held three times a year; small markets
on Saturdays.

Restoration Hardware
935 Broadway
New York, NY 10011
212 260 9479
www.restorationhardware.com
Not just hardware, also home
furnishings, lighting and home and
garden accessories.

Ruby Beets Antiques
1703 Montauk Highway
Bridgehampton, NY 11932
516 537 2802
Nineteenth- and early-twentieth-century
furniture, decorative objects, paintings.

Saks Fifth Avenue
call 800 347 9177 for store locations
High-quality women's fashions,
including pashmina shawls; mail order.

Scott Antique Market
Atlanta Exposition Center
3650 Jonesboro Road
Atlanta, GA 30354
call 740 569 4112 for dates
Markets, held over three days, once a
month. Some 2,500 stalls selling a vast
array of antiques, from junk to treasures.

Silk Trading Company
360 S. La Brea Avenue
Los Angeles, CA 90036
323 954 9280
Silk furnishing fabrics.

The Tomato Factory
2 Somerset Street
Hopewell, NJ 09525
609 466 9833
Cooperative of 31 antique dealers
offering everything from fine period
furniture to transferware and rag rugs.

Waterworks
29 Park Avenue
Danbury, CT 06820
800 899 6757 or 203 792 9979
Importers of old-style bathroom fixtures;
also some modern styles; mail order.

Williams Sonoma
call 800 541 2233 (for orders) or 800
541 1262 (for customer service)
www.williams-sonoma.com
Chain with stores in many cities,
selling kitchenware, table linens,
appliances, and more; mail order.

architects and designers whose work is featured in this book

Key: **t** = top, **b** = below, **c** = center,
l = left, **r** = right

Ken Foreman
Architect
105 Duane Street
New York, NY 10007
tel & fax 212 924 4503
Pages 9, 16, 60 **l**, 62, 63 **tr**, 94, 120,
128 **tr**, **cr** & **br**, 129

Belmont Freeman Architects
Project team: Belmont Freeman
(Principal designer), Alane Truitt,
Sangho Park
110 West 40th Street
New York, NY 10018
212 382 3311

fax 212 730 1229
Pages 22 **l**, 51 **tr** & **br**, 60 **r**, 61, 63 **l**,
95 **b**, 104-105, 120-121, 128 **l**

Jacksons
5 All Saints Road
London W11 1HA
England
+44 (0)20 7792 8336
Pages 12-13, 64, 82 **l**, 110 **bl** & **br**

Daniel Jasiak
Designer
12 rue Jean Ferrandi
Paris 75006
France
+33 (0)1 45 49 13 56
fax +33 (0)1 45 49 23 66
Pages 7 **r**, 19, 37, 69 **tc**, 74, 75 **l**,
76, 86 **bc**, 90 **r**, 91, 131 **tl** & **r**,
132 **c** & **r**, 133

Lena Proudlock
Furniture Design
Gloucestershire GL8 8UN
England
Pages 25 **t**, 65, 82 **r**, 92, 111, 114 **b**,
115, 118 **l**, 126 **b**, 127 **tl** & **tr**

Ann Shore
London-based designer & stylist
tel & fax +44 (0)20 7377 6377
Pages 7 **l**, 8 **r**, 18 **r**, 29, 32 **r**, 33, 36, 75
r, 86 **tl** & **br**, 87, 89 **l** & **br**, 108, 109 **tr**,
130, 131 **bl**, 132 **l**, 136-137, 138-139

27.12 Design Ltd.
451 Greenwich Street
Suite 504
New York, NY 10013
212 334 5245
Pages 48 **bl**, 50, 51 **bl**, 93 **l** & **br**, 106

index

Page numbers in italic refer to the photographs

picture credits

Key: **t** = top, **b**= below, **l** = left, **r** = right, **c** = center

Endpapers Clare Nash's house in London; 1 Mary Foley's house in Connecticut; 2-3 Adria Ellis' apartment in New York; 6 Clare Nash's house in London; 7 **l** Ann Shore's house in London; 7 **c** Mary Foley's house in Connecticut; 7 **r** Daniel Jasiak's apartment in Paris; 8 **l** & **c** Liz Stirling's apartment in Paris; 8 **r** Ann Shore's house in London; 9 Kathy Moskal's apartment in New York designed by Ken Foreman; 12–13 Louise Jackson's house in London; 14–15 Clare Nash's house in London; 16 Kathy Moskal's apartment in New York designed by Ken Foreman; 18 **l** Clare Nash's house in London; 18 **r** Ann Shore's house in London; 19 Daniel Jasiak's apartment in Paris; 20 Ros Fairman's house in London; 21 Mary Foley's house in Connecticut; 22 **l** an apartment in New York designed by Belmont Freeman Architects; 25 **t** Lena Proudlock's house in Gloucestershire; 26 Ros Fairman's house in London; 27 **tl** & **br** Ros Fairman's house in London; 27 **tr** Adria Ellis' apartment in New York; 29 Ann Shore's house in London; 30 & 30-31 Kimberley Watson's house in London; 31 **r** Ros Fairman's house in London; 32 **l** Liz Stirling's apartment in Paris; 32 **r** & 33 Ann Shore's house in London; 34 Liz Stirling's apartment in Paris; 35 **tl** & **br** Liz Stirling's apartment in Paris; 36 Ann Shore's house in London; 37 Daniel Jasiak's apartment in Paris; 38 Carol Reid's apartment in Paris; 39 **tl** Glenn Carwithen & Sue Miller's house in London; 39 **b** Carol Reid's apartment in Paris; 40-41 Ros Fairman's house in London; 42 Ros Fairman's house in London; 43 Clare Nash's house in London; 44 Marie-Hélène de Taillac's pied-à-terre in Paris; 46 **tr** Kimberley Watson's house in London; 47 Marie-Hélène de Taillac's pied-à-terre in Paris; 48 **bl** Home of 27.12 Design Ltd., Chelsea, NYC; 48 **r** & 49 Glenn Carwithen & Sue Miller's house in London; 50 & 51 **bl** Home of 27.12 Design Ltd., Chelsea, NYC; 51 **tr** & **br** an apartment in New York designed by Belmont Freeman Architects; 52-53 The Sawmills Studios; 54-55 Marie-Hélène de Taillac's pied-à-terre in Paris; 56-57 Glenn Carwithen & Sue Miller's house in London; 58 **l** Glenn Carwithen & Sue Miller's house in London; 58 **r** & 59 Mary Foley's house in Connecticut; 60 **l** Courtney Brennan's apartment in New York designed by Ken Foreman; 60 **r** & 61 an apartment in New York designed by Belmont Freeman Architects; 62 Kathy Moskal's apartment in New York designed by Ken Foreman; 63 **l** an apartment in New York designed by Belmont Freeman Architects; 63 **tr** Kathy Moskal's apartment in New York designed by Ken Foreman; 64 Louise Jackson's house in London; 65 Lena Proudlock's house in Gloucestershire; 66-67 Carol Reid's apartment in Paris; 68 Clare Nash's house in London; 69 **tl** & **b** Kimberley Watson's house in London; 69 **tc** Daniel Jasiak's apartment in Paris; 69 **tr** Clare Nash's house in London; 70 **l** & 71 **tl** Clare Nash's house in London; 70 **r** & 71 **r** Mary Foley's house in Connecticut; 72 **l** Adria Ellis' apartment in New York; 73 The Sawmills Studios; 74 & 75 **l** Daniel Jasiak's apartment in Paris; 75 **r** Ann Shore's house in London; 76 Daniel Jasiak's apartment in Paris; 77 **tl** Adria Ellis' apartment in New York; 77 **tr** Kimberley Watson's house in London; 77 **bl** & **br** Mary Foley's house in Connecticut; 78-79 Kimberley Watson's house in London; 80-81 Glenn Carwithen & Sue Miller's house in London; 82 **l** Louise Jackson's house in London; 82 **r** Lena Proudlock's house in Gloucestershire; 83 The Sawmills Studios; 84-85 Ros Fairman's house in London; 86 **tl** & **br** Ann Shore's house in London; 86 **tr**, **c** & **bl** Clare Nash's house in London; 86 **bc** Daniel Jasiak's apartment in Paris; 87 Ann Shore's house in London; 88 Carol Reid's apartment in Paris; 89 **l** & **br** Ann Shore's house in London; 89 **tr** Glenn Carwithen & Sue Miller's house in London, painting by Alan Grimwood; 90 **l** The Sawmills Studios; 90 **r** & 91 Daniel Jasiak's apartment in Paris; 92 Lena Proudlock's house in Gloucestershire; 93 **l** & **br** Home of 27.12 Design Ltd., Chelsea, NYC; 93 **tr** Marie-Hélène de Taillac's pied-à-terre in Paris; 93 **cr** Adria Ellis' apartment in New York; 94 Courtney Brennan's apartment in New York designed by Ken Foreman; 95 **t** Kimberley Watson's house in London; 95 **b** an apartment in New York designed by Belmont Freeman Architects; 96-97 Ros Fairman's house in London; 98-99 The Sawmills Studios; 100 Mary Foley's house in Connecticut; 101 Adria Ellis' apartment in New York, painting by Peter Zangrillo; 103 Kimberley Watson's house in London; 104-105 an apartment in New York designed by Belmont Freeman Architects; 106 Home of 27.12 Design Ltd., Chelsea, NYC; 107 Glenn Carwithen & Sue Miller's house in London; 108 Ann Shore's house in London; 109 **bl** & **c** Ros Fairman's house in London; 109 **tr** Ann Shore's house in London; 109 **br** Adria Ellis' apartment in New York; 110 **t** Marie-Hélène de Taillac's pied-à-terre in Paris; 110 **bl** & **br** Louise Jackson's house in London; 111 Lena Proudlock's house in Gloucestershire; 112-113 Ros Fairman's house in London; 114 **t** Carol Reid's apartment in Paris; 114 **b** & 115 Lena Proudlock's house in Gloucestershire; 116 **t** & **c** Kimberley Watson's house in London; 116 **b** The Sawmills Studios; 117 Kimberley Watson's house in London; 118 **l** Lena Proudlock's house in Gloucestershire; 118 **r** Mary Foley's house in Connecticut; 119 Carol Reid's apartment in Paris; 120 Kathy Moskal's apartment in New York designed by Ken Foreman; 120-121 an apartment in New York designed by Belmont Freeman Architects; 122-123 The Sawmills Studios; 126 **t** Marie-Hélène de Taillac's pied-à-terre in Paris; 126 **b** Lena Proudlock's house in Gloucestershire; 127 **tl** & **tr** Lena Proudlock's house in Gloucestershire; 127 **bl** & **br** Marie-Hélène de Taillac's pied-à-terre in Paris; 128 **l** an apartment in New York designed by Belmont Freeman Architects; 128 **tr** Kathy Moskal's apartment in New York designed by Ken Foreman; 128 **cr** & **br** Courtney Brennan's apartment in New York designed by Ken Foreman; 129 Kathy Moskal's apartment in New York designed by Ken Foreman; 130 & 131 **bl** Ann Shore's house in London; 131 **tl** & **r** Daniel Jasiak's apartment in Paris; 132 **l** Ann Shore's house in London; 132 **c** & **r** & 133 Daniel Jasiak's apartment in Paris; 134 Mary Foley's house in Connecticut; 136 Mary Foley's house in Connecticut; 136-137 Ann Shore's house in London; 137 **r** Mary Foley's house in Connecticut; 138-139 Ann Shore's house in London; 140 Carol Reid's apartment in Paris

acknowledgments

First, I would like to say a huge thank-you to Polly Wreford for her dedication and visual insight; for consistently taking such exquisite pictures, and for keeping us all smiling with her infectious laugh. Also, thanks to Matt Wrixon for his good humor and hard work, and of course to Gloria Daniel for her boundless energy and support. I could not have wished for a better team.

Thanks to Alice Westgate for her unfailing assistance in ensuring that the text was written on time, and to everyone at Ryland Peters & Small, especially Anne Ryland and Gabriella Le Grazie, for giving me such a wonderful opportunity. I would also like to thank Kate Brunt and Hilary Mandleberg for their much-needed help, and Vicky Holmes for the book's beautiful design.

But most of all, thanks to Dave for his inspiration, encouragement, and for generally being fantastic.